Christian Festival Tales

written by

Saviour Pirotta

illustrated by

Helen Cann

Hodder
Wayland

an imprint of Hodder Children's Books

Festival Tales

Christian Festival Tales • Hindu Festival Tales
Jewish Festival Tales • Muslim Festival Tales

© 2000 White-Thomson Publishing Ltd
Text copyright © Saviour Pirotta 2000

Produced for Hodder Wayland by
White-Thomson Publishing Ltd
2/3 St Andrew's Place
Lewes BN7 1UP

Series concept: Saviour Pirotta/Philippa Smith/Polly Goodman
Editor: Margot Richardson
Designer: Jane Hawkins
Music score: John Nicholson

Published in Great Britain by Hodder Wayland, a division of Hodder Children's Books
First published in paperback in 2001
The right of Saviour Pirotta to be identified as the author and Helen Cann as the illustrator
of this Work has been asserted by them in accordance with
the Copyright, Designs and Patents Act 1988.

A Catalogue record for this book is available from the British Library.

ISBN 0 7502 3257 9

Printed and bound in Italy by EUROGRAFICA S.p.A., Marano Vic.

Hodder Children's Books
a division of Hodder Headline Limited
338 Euston Road, London NW1 3BH

Contents

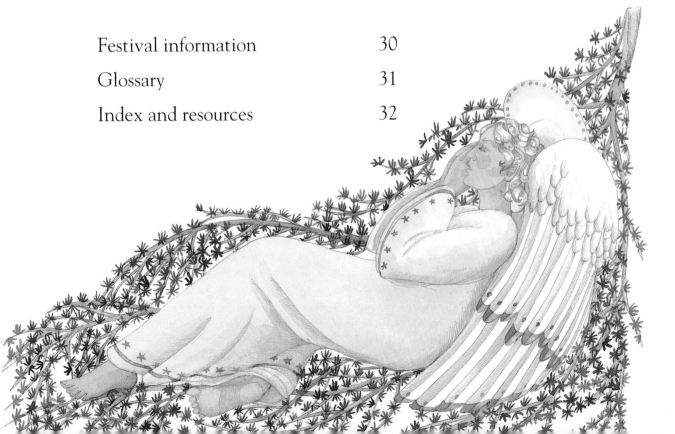

La Befana

The first festival of the Christian year takes place on the sixth of January. It is called Epiphany and marks the day when the three wise men finally got to see Jesus in his manger. This Epiphany story is from Italy.

Befana was a lonely old woman. She lived alone in a little house, just a few miles down the road from the village of Bethlehem. Sadly, no one ever came to visit her. So Befana spent most of her days on her own, wishing she had someone to keep her company.

One day, Befana heard a clattering outside the house. She looked out of the window and saw a long line of travellers coming down the road. People did not often pass by, so she went out to have a closer look.

The travellers were all riding camels. Three of them had crowns on their heads and were dressed in beautiful clothes. They were obviously kings from faraway countries.

'Is this the way to Bethlehem?' asked one of the three kings.

'It is indeed,' said Befana, dazzled by the kings' splendour.

'We are looking for a new-born baby, who is a king,' said the second king. 'Have you heard of him?'

'I'm afraid I haven't,' said Befana wistfully. She loved children, especially babies. Many times, she wished she'd had children of her own so she wouldn't be so lonely now.

'Why don't you come with us?' said the third king. 'We have been following that bright star up there, for a long time now. It has stopped over Bethlehem. We are sure the baby king is there.'

Befana looked up at the star. 'I wish I could come,' she said, 'but I have a lot to do. I can't just leave.'

'Perhaps you can catch up with us later,' said the king kindly.

The long line of travellers continued along the road. Befana went indoors and started cleaning the stove. But she could not get the idea of the new-born king out of her head. How I'd like to see that baby, she thought. Just one peek and I'll come back home.

After a while, Befana stood up and wiped her hands on her apron. She had made up her mind. It was almost night, but she was going to see the baby.

And she was going to take him some gifts as well. Befana kept a few toys in the house, just in case someone with children dropped by. She put them in a sack and hurried down the road, keeping an eye out for the kings and their followers.

Befana walked and walked, but she could not catch up with the three kings. Towards morning, she reached Bethlehem. 'Have you seen the new-born king?' she asked some shepherds.

'We have,' they said, 'but he and his parents have moved on.'

'Which way did they go?' asked Befana.

'That way,' said the shepherds, pointing down a long road.

Befana hurried down the road, but she never found Baby Jesus. Time passed and she kept going on, from village to village, from town to town and from country to country.

'How wonderful the world is,' she said, 'and what interesting people I have met on my travels! I shall never go back home to my lonely little house by the roadside.'

And, strange to say, the old woman is wandering still. She gives out presents too. Every Epiphany, at night, she visits many houses and leaves toys and books in children's stockings, just in case one of them is a new king or queen.

8

Shrove Tuesday

This day is known as Pancake Day in some countries. In the past it was the last opportunity for people to have fun and eat rich foods before fasting for Lent. Many people made pancakes to use up their last eggs. Today, very few people fast, but many still have pancakes as a treat.

Mix a Pancake

Mix a pancake
Stir a pancake
Pop it in a pan

Fry the pancake
Toss the pancake
Catch it if you can

Christina Rossetti

Pancake Recipe
Makes 8 pancakes

100 g plain flour
275 ml milk

1 egg
Oil for frying

1 Mix the egg and some of the milk with the flour until smooth.
2 Beat in the rest of the milk.
3 Heat a little oil in the pan until it is sizzling hot.
4 Pour in some of the mixture and swirl it around until it covers the pan.
5 When the pancake is brown on the bottom and dry on the top side, turn or toss it over.
6 Serve the pancakes with sugar and lemon juice; honey and fruit; or stuffed with tuna and sweetcorn.

WARNING: do not cook pancakes without an adult's help. Oil will get very hot and could burn you.

The Obstinate Donkey

Palm Sunday marks the day when Jesus entered Jerusalem, hailed by crowds waving palm branches. It is also the start of Holy Week, which finishes with Easter.

The farmer was angry. His donkey, which was costing him a fortune in oats and hay, would not do any work. It wouldn't even carry a bundle on its back.

'I'm going to have that stupid beast put down,' said the farmer angrily. But his children begged him not to kill it.

'Give it away,' said his wife. 'Someone will find it a home.'

The farmer tied the donkey to a post outside his farm. 'Whoever wants the stupid creature is welcome to it,' he said out loud.

Two men happened to be passing by. 'Can we really take it?' they asked.

'You may,' said the farmer, 'but I have to warn you: it refuses to carry anything.'

The two men took the donkey to Jesus, their leader. Jesus was going to Jerusalem, to pray at the temple for the Passover feast.

'We have brought the donkey you requested,' said the two disciples, 'but the farmer who gave it to us says it refuses to carry anything.'

'You can't enter Jerusalem on a donkey,' said another disciple. 'Why don't you ride a horse? There are lots of people who would lend you one.'

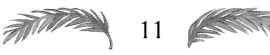

But Jesus only wanted the donkey. He whispered something in its right ear. The donkey brayed, then it let him climb on to its back. 'There,' said Jesus, 'this noble creature is good enough for me.'

The donkey was very proud to hear Jesus calling it 'noble'. Other people had only ever called it 'stupid' or 'obstinate' before. It carried Jesus into the city, holding its head up high and its ears straight. The crowds cheered Jesus on, waving palm branches to show that they recognized him as their king.

When Jesus reached the temple, he climbed down and patted the donkey on the back. 'Thank you,' he said politely.

The donkey brayed with joy. And ever since, some donkeys have carried the mark of the cross on their back, to show that one of their ancestors had once carried Jesus.

The Angel's Gift

There are many stories about Good Friday.
Many of them are about the cross on which Jesus
was crucified. In some, certain trees share in Christ's
suffering by having their wood used for the cross.

An angel came flying across the stormy countryside, his golden wings dripping with rain.

'Cedar,' he called out to a young tree, 'may I shelter under your branches?'

'By all means,' said the cedar, and she wrapped her tender branches around him. Thunder rolled and lightning forked across the sky. The angel trembled.

'Go to sleep,' whispered the cedar, comforting him. 'I'll wake you up when the storm has passed.'

The angel closed his eyes and went to sleep. When the tree woke him again, the storm had waned and the sun was shining.

'Thank you, Cedar,' said the angel. 'May your fruit be a blessing to the whole world.' And, with that, he flew up into the heavens.

Years passed and the young cedar grew into a mighty tree. Her branches were strong and solid, but she bore no fruit for people to eat. Sometimes, when birds had gone to sleep in her branches, she remembered what the angel had said to her: 'May your fruit be a blessing to the whole world.'

'But how can that be?' she wondered. 'How can my fruit be a blessing if I bear none?'

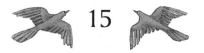

Then, one day, three soldiers came along the road, each one wielding an axe. 'This will do,' said one, pointing to the cedar. They raised their axes and, in no time at all, the mighty tree crashed to the ground. The soldiers lopped off most of her branches, then they dragged her to a palace. There, they placed her on the shoulders of a condemned man.

The poor man was in pain. Blood was pouring down his face. The soldiers forced him to carry his burden up a steep hill. Crowds of people followed, some crying, others jeering.

At the top of the hill, the soldiers nailed the man to the cedar. As they raised up the tree, a terrible storm broke loose on the world, tearing the countryside to pieces.

The man sighed one last time and died. The tree
moaned, numbed with pain and fear. But suddenly,
her old friend the angel was by her side.

'The man who hangs from your branches is the
Son of God,' he said. 'His death has saved mankind
and opened the doors to heaven. Behold, the fruit of
your pain is a blessing to all.'

Then the cedar understood. She had been chosen;
she would be remembered forever as the tree that
helped to save the world.

Were you there when they Crucified my Lord?

This is a traditional 'negro spiritual': a song that was
originally sung by Black American people many years ago.
It is a very simple telling of the Easter story.

Were you there when they cru - ci - fied my

Lord? _____ Were you there when they

cru - ci - fied my Lord? _____

Oh! _____ Some-times it cau - ses me to

trem - ble, trem - ble, trem - ble. Were you

there when they cru - ci - fied my Lord? _____

2 Were you there when they nailed him to the tree?
  Were you there when they nailed him to the tree?
Oh! Sometimes it causes me to tremble, tremble, tremble
  Were you there when they nailed him to the tree?

3 Were you there when the sun refused to shine?
  Were you there when the sun refused to shine?
Oh! Sometimes it causes me to tremble, tremble, tremble
  Were you there when the sun refused to shine?

4 Were you there when they laid him in the tomb?
  Were you there when they laid him in the tomb?
Oh! Sometimes it causes me to tremble, tremble, tremble
  Were you there when they laid him in the tomb?

5 Were you there when God raised him from the dead?
  Were you there when God raised him from the dead?
Oh! Sometimes it causes me to sing glory, glory, glory!
  Were you there when God raised him from the dead?

Tongues of Fire

Here is the story of Pentecost, or Whit Sunday, which takes place on the fiftieth day after Easter. It is considered to be the birthday of the church, because it was the first time that Jesus' disciples started preaching about him.

On the fiftieth day after Easter Sunday, Jesus' disciples were all gathered in the room where they had shared the Last Supper with him. A great Jewish festival called Pentecost was about to begin and the streets of Jerusalem were packed with people.

'Now's the perfect time to tell everyone about Jesus and his teachings,' said an old disciple.

'It is, indeed,' agreed another. But no one had the courage to go out and start preaching. Somehow, they all felt a bit lost without the Master.

Suddenly, a strong wind blew around the house, rattling the shutters in the windows. Tongues of flame appeared in the air. All at once the men were filled with the Holy Spirit. They felt strong and full of courage. Some of them began to speak in strange languages they had never even heard before.

The flames winked out and disappeared. But the spirit remained with the disciples. They rushed outside and started telling people all about Jesus and the things he had taught them. The crowds were amazed, for here were simple fishermen, talking in foreign languages like learned men.

More than three thousand people came to believe in Jesus that day. And thousands more were soon to follow, for the brave disciples spread far and wide, telling everyone they met about the holy Saviour.

Pentecost Prayer

Alleluia, alleluia
Come, holy Spirit, fill our hearts
with the fire of your love!
Alleluia

The Magnificent Little Fir Tree

A Christmas play

Christmas celebrates the birth of Jesus Christ. It is a popular festival that, for many people, is the highlight of the year. Here's a play you can perform during your Christmas celebrations at school. It's based on an ancient folk tale.

Cast of Characters

An olive tree   Angel 1

A palm tree   Shepherds

A little fir tree   Other angels

Joshua, an inn-keeper

Joseph, a carpenter from Nazareth

Mary, his wife

Scene: An inn outside Bethlehem

When the lights come on, we see an archway leading into a dark Mediterranean stable. Through the door we can just about make out a pile of hay but not much else. To the right of the stable is an inn, with a door and a small window. To the left of it stand the Palm, the Olive and, further back, the Little Fir Tree. The trees are actors dressed in green, with branches on their heads to distinguish them from one another.

Olive [yawning]: It is so boring out here in Bethlehem. I wish I lived right next to the king's palace in Jerusalem. Then I could see everything that goes on in court.

Palm: I wish I lived in an oasis. I'd be standing right next to a shimmering lake.

Fir [hesitantly]: I quite like it here.

The Olive and The Palm shake their heads in exasperation.

Olive: You would. You're just a common fir tree.

Palm [chuckling]: It stinks around here.

Olive [laughing]: Of goat's droppings.

Enter Joseph, who knocks at the door of the inn.

Palm [whispering]: Who's that?

Olive: A thief, probably.

Fir: He doesn't look like a thief.

Olive: Well, you've got to admit, Bethlehem is crawling with thieves.

The door opens and Joshua the innkeeper comes out.

Joseph [very politely]: Excuse me, Mr. Innkeeper, but do you have any spare rooms at the inn?

Joshua: I'm afraid we've got no vacancies tonight. Try the tavern down the road.

Joseph: I've tried there already. They're full. I don't know what to do. My wife's about to have her baby...

Joshua: Your wife is having a baby? You can't go wandering around town in this weather, then. Look, why don't you spend the night in my stable? It's clean, and I won't charge you anything.

Joseph: That's very kind of you, Mr. Innkeeper. I'll fetch my wife at once. She's waiting by the road. My name's Joseph, by the way. My wife's called Mary.

Joshua: And I'm Joshua. I'll fetch you a light and some blankets.

Joseph exits stage right. Joshua goes back into the inn.

Olive [to Palm]: Did you hear that? A woman's having a baby, right here, in the stable.

Palm: Something like this would never happen in an oasis. People are more refined there. They have their babies at home.

Olive: Ssh, be quiet Palm! Someone's coming.

25

The trees stand still. Joshua comes out of the inn with blankets and a lantern. He carries the things into the stable. A moment later Joseph leads Mary onstage.

Joseph: Look Mary, I've found us a dry stable.

Joshua comes out to greet them.

Joshua: I hope it'll be warm enough. I've put some blankets in the manger for the baby. Knock on my door if you need any more.
Mary: Thank you very much, Joshua.
Joshua: I'll say goodnight, then.
Mary/Joseph: Goodnight.

Joshua goes into the inn and closes the door. Joseph and Mary go into the stables.

Palm: I wonder what they're going to call the baby.
Olive: Barabbas, I shouldn't wonder. All thugs seem to be called Barabbas nowadays.
Fir: Joseph and Mary don't look like thieves.
Palm [disdainfully]: What would you know about it? You're only a common Fir.

Suddenly there is a loud fanfare of trumpets. A bright light shines in the sky.

Olive: What's going on? Who lit that bright torch at this time of night?

Enter a host of angels, lead by Angel 1.

Angel 1: Rejoice, for here is the Messiah, the King of Kings, born in a stable.

All the angels except Angel 1 enter the stable. A moment later the shepherds burst onstage. They all bear gifts.

Shepherd 1: Is he here, the Messiah, the King of Kings?
Angel 1: He lies in yonder stable.

Shepherd: We bear humble gifts: oil and figs, wine for the father, a warm shawl for the Christ-child.

They all follow the angels into the stable.

Olive: Did you hear that? A king, born right here in our stable.

Palm: We must give him a gift right away.

Olive: Yes, I'll give him one of my branches. Kings are always anointed with olive oil, you know.

Palm: And I'll give him a palm leaf. His mother can fan him with it.

Fir: What can I give Baby Jesus? I know, I'll give him some of my needles.

Olive and Palm laugh cruelly.

Palm: Don't you dare drop those dangerous things around the king. He might prick his royal fingers on them.

Olive: Stay away from his majesty. Leave these royal occasions to us, the nobility.

The Fir shrinks away from the stable and stands still. Enter the First Angel.

Angel 1: Come, behold the Saviour, the King of Kings. [*He sees the Fir Tree.*] Why do you stand there, so sad and alone? Rejoice, for the Messiah is born!

Fir: I, er, don't want to drop needles near Baby Jesus.

Angel 1: That's very thoughtful of you, little tree.

He claps, and the other angels run out of the stable. They all hang stars on the Fir's branches.

Palm [to Olive]: That's not fair. I should be the one covered in stars.

Olive: You should be covered in dates, dear. I am the one who should be decked with glittering constellations.

The shepherds come out of the stable.

Shepherd 1: Look at that marvellous little tree. It's covered in stars.

Shepherd 2: It's beautiful.

Shepherd 3: It's a sign that light has entered our lives.

Angel 1: Remember this tree, for like Baby Jesus it is meek and humble. And yet its kindness has made it the most magnificent tree in the world. Behold, the very first Christmas tree!

Music. The children deck the little Fir tree with decorations and tinsel. Then the shepherds dance around it.

Festival Information

Christians believe that there are three persons in one God: God the Father, God the Son and the Holy Spirit. When people fell out of grace with God, God the son became a man, Jesus of Nazareth, to save them, by dying on the cross. Most Christian festivals celebrate important dates in the life of Jesus and the people around him.

EPIPHANY is also called Twelfth Night, as it falls on sixth of January. Originally linked to Christ's baptism, it now marks the day when the three wise men from the Orient presented the infant Jesus with myrrh, gold and frankincense. In many countries, it is the greatest celebration of the Christmas season. In Spain, for example, three men dressed as the Magi travel around town or village on horseback. They are followed by their servants and shepherds who shower passers-by with sweets.

In the Orthodox Churches, Epiphany is celebrated with the blessing of water. During the ceremony, a priest throws a cross into the water to remind people about Jesus' baptism in the river Jordan. In hot countries, the ceremony is often conducted by the sea, and children dive into the water to retrieve the cross.

SHROVE TUESDAY This is the last day of indulgence before the start of Lent, which lasts for 40 days (excluding Sundays), until Easter. In many countries, Shrove Tuesday comes straight after carnival, traditionally a time of feasting and merrymaking.

ASH WEDNESDAY is the day after Shrove Tuesday, and is the beginning of Lent. During a special ceremony, a priest marks people's foreheads with a cross made of ashes and holy water, as a reminder that man is mortal and will one day have to die.

PALM SUNDAY comes at the beginning of the Easter Holy Week. It celebrates the day when Jesus entered Jerusalem on a donkey and was greeted by crowds waving palm branches. Churches are decorated with palm fronds and sometimes willow branches. People take part in processions between churches or along village streets. Many carry palm fronds woven into crosses, or olive branches.

After the ceremony, the palm and olive branches are burnt and the ashes kept for next year's Ash Wednesday.

GOOD FRIDAY is two days before Easter Sunday. It marks the day when Jesus died on the cross. It is called 'Good' Friday because Christians believe that Christ's death saved mankind and opened the doors to heaven. It is a holy day of obligation, with many people fasting and eating no meat. Children refrain from eating sweets and puddings. Traditional Good Friday foods include hot cross buns in England, pumpkin and bean soup in Malta and lentil and vinegar soup in Cyprus.

In many countries, Catholic Churches are draped in black. Paintings and statues are covered over as a sign of mourning. Pageants and processions are held in towns and villages where statues showing the story of Christ's death are carried through the streets.

EASTER SUNDAY is the most important day in the Christian calendar. It does not fall on a set date, but may be any Sunday between 22nd March and 25th April. Easter celebrates the day when Jesus rose from the dead. Easter also marks the end of Lent and the culmination of Holy Week. Special Masses and outdoor ceremonies are held all over the world. During the Mass, the priest lights a huge candle to show that Christ is risen and that He is the light of the world. In some countries, a statue of the risen Christ is carried along the streets. The mood of this procession is very different from that of Good Friday. People cheer as the statue is carried past their homes and local bands play joyous music.

Easter comes in Spring. Many believe that the early Christians started celebrating Easter instead of an older, pre-Christian festival celebrating the rebirth of Mother Nature. The word 'Easter' is an adaptation of Eostre, the name of the Anglo-Saxon goddess of Spring.

Eggs, the symbol of rebirth, are a popular Easter gift. In some cultures, relatives exchange biscuits in the shape of lambs. They are often covered in icing sugar and decorated with a small chocolate egg. There are Easter breads and cakes too.

WHIT SUNDAY comes seven weeks after Easter. It is also called Pentecost, or Whitsun, and marks the day when Christ's disciples were filled with the Holy Spirit and preached to the public for the first time. Many consider it to be the birthday of the church. Pentecost is also the Jewish festival of Shavuot.

THE FEAST OF SAINT PETER AND SAINT PAUL is always celebrated on the 29th June. Saint Peter and Saint Paul are two of the most important saints in the Christian religion. Saint Peter was one of the original twelve apostles. Saint Paul was a Jewish man who became a Christian and was the first to welcome non-Jewish people to the new religion.

HARVEST FESTIVAL is people's way of thanking God for food and comforts. In Britain, it is usually celebrated during October. People donate food which is then given out to the needy or the old. In America the harvest festival is called Thanksgiving and takes place on the fourth Thursday of November. A traditional meal of roast turkey is eaten.

CHRISTMAS celebrates the day when Jesus was born in a stable in Bethlehem, a small village outside Jerusalem in present-day Israel. Christmas is celebrated with prayers, special ceremonies, the exchanging of presents and cards, good food and decorations.
  Traditional Christmas food varies from country to country but everyone seems to have a Christmas cake. In Denmark, it is flavoured with ground almonds, while Italian children have a very light sponge cake called Panettone. It comes with a small packet of icing sugar which you dust on to each slice before you eat it.
  For many Christians the highlight of the Christmas celebrations is the midnight Mass or carol service.

Glossary

Alleluia A word that means 'praise to God'.

Brayed Made a donkey's 'hee-haw' sound.

Constellations Groups of stars in the sky.

Crucified Put to death by being fastened to a cross.

Disciple Someone who followed Jesus.

Fast To not eat food, or some kinds of food.

Holy Sacred, belonging to God.

Holy Spirit The third of the three 'persons' that are in God.

Last Supper The last meal eaten by Jesus and his followers, the night before Jesus died on the cross.

Messiah A person who is expected to save a country from its enemies.

Negro A name that used to be given to black people, especially Black Americans, whose ancestors originally came from Africa.

Obstinate Will not do what anyone else wants.

Oasis A fertile place in the middle of a desert, with water, trees and plants.

Passover A Jewish spring festival.

Preach Make a speech about religious ideas and beliefs.

Saviour A person who saves someone or something from being destroyed.

Tomb A cave or building where a dead person's body is kept.

Tremble Shaking, caused by being afraid or excited.

Vacancies Space or rooms for people to stay in.

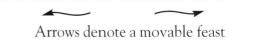
Arrows denote a movable feast

August

July

May
Whit Sunday

June
29th – Feast of St Peter & St Paul

Index

Resources

Books

Easter, Catherine Chambers (Evans Bros, 1997). Learn all about Easter around the world.

Feasting for Festivals, Jan Wilson (Lion, 1990). Customs and recipes to celebrate the Christian year.

The First Christmas, The National Gallery (Frances Lincoln, 1992). The Christmas story illustrated with paintings from the National Gallery.

Good Friday Liturgy for Young Children, Barbara Mary Hooper and the Benedict Nuns Of Turvery Abbey (McCrimmon, 1997).

Harvest, Clare Chandler (Wayland, 1997). Information about the festival's origins and a map showing where in the world it is celebrated.

The Orchard Christmas Treasury, Sally Emerson (Orchard Books, 1994). Christmas food, legends, songs and activities.

Stories from the Christian World, Sheena Vickers (Macdonald Young Books, 1998). Wonderful stories about the Christian faith.

Videos

The Greatest Story Ever Told, a magnificent film about Good Friday and Easter. Stars Max Von Sydow as Christ.

Godspell, a fresh look at the story of Jesus with music and dancing.

The Robe, a fictional account of what happened to Jesus' miraculous robe after his death. With Richard Burton, Jean Simmons and Victor Mature.

Ben Hur, the story of two friends, one of whom witnesses the death of Christ. Features a spectacular chariot race and a dramatic sea battle. Stars Charlton Heston.

Web sites

www.chenowith.k12.or.us/tech/subject/fun/easter.html
 'Easter on the net': activites and stories for children
www.95church.com/index.html
 Details of Christmas and Easter plays that children can perform.
www.geocities.com/heartland/7134/christmas/chrstories.htm
 Christmas and related stories for children, with music.